D1291967

THE

SPIRIT

AND

SPIRITUALITY

(Second Edition)

by
J. D. Thomas

Published By
BIBLICAL RESEARCH PRESS
1334 RUSWOOD
ABILENE, TEXAS
79601

THE SPIRIT AND SPIRITUALTY

(SECOND EDITION)

by J. D. Thomas

◆

Copyright © 1981, by
Biblical Research Press

◆

Library of Congress Catalog Card No. 81-68342
ISBN — 0-89112-121-8

◆

First Printing — 1966
Fourth Printing — 1981

PREFACE

Due to the success of this little booklet since its first publication, we have decided to revise it as to more precise wording at certain points, and to implement its usefulness by adding study questions at the end of each chapter to further sharpen consideration of the issues.

Since we feel that it will have an enduring life we have reset the type to make it more readable and attractive and we believe the new format will be appreciated.

The ideas herein presented have had their share of opposition, but we believe that they have not really been answered in the light of scriptural teachings, so we have no lack of confidence in the basic thrust of the booklet and are glad to offer this revised version.

Abilene
Summer 1981

CONTENTS

Chapter 1

THE HOLY SPIRIT

Ever so often Christians "hit a snag" in their collective thinking and what had before not been a problem becomes one. This has recently become true for some about the interpretation of the teaching of the New Testament concerning the influence of the Holy Spirit in the life of today's Christian. In studying out this problem, Christians should be careful to be kind and considerate of each other and to count each other as sincere and earnest seekers of truth. Only with loving attitudes can we carry on an adequate discussion. This study is offered in this spirit, and we hope that someone will in due brotherly kindness help us to arrive at the real truth about any point where we mistake the true meaning of the New Testament.

Only the New Testament itself can be authority for instructing about God's will for us today. There is no other basis for establishing religious truth. We cannot, for example, accept private experience or testimony as establishing public religious truth, valid and binding upon all. And, unless we can prove our points from the New Testament itself we also find it in vain to cite "previous *church fathers*" or even current or recent interpreters. Human tradition is not authority, and controversial issues must be settled by the New Testament and not by what "brother so and so" has taught.

As near as we possibly can, the teaching on this important matter should be "spelled out" clearly for all who want to know. It should be systematized and organized logically in its presentation so that the plain Christian can know with a degree of assurance that he understands the New Testament teaching about the Holy Spirit.

The Nature of the Holy Spirit

The Holy Spirit is a person, the third member of the Godhead, thus He is equated with the Father and the Son (Matt. 28:19). The personal pronouns "He" and "Him" are clearly used of the Holy Spirit in John 14:16, 17, and 26, and the Greek language is definite in such designations. Thus in the same way that God is a personal spirit-being and Christ is a personal spirit-being, so also is the Holy Spirit. He should therefore properly be referred to as "He" and not as "it". His personality is further confirmed by the New Testament passages which represent Him as capable of experiencing emotions — Eph. 4:30 "do not *grieve* the Holy Spirit of God"; Heb. 10:29 "has regarded as unclean the blood of the covenant by which he was sanctified, and has *insulted* (done despite unto, ARV) the Spirit of grace?; James 4:5 (margin) "The Spirit which He has made to dwell in us *jealously desires* us"; Rom. 8:26 "the Spirit Himself (intensive pronoun) *intercedes* for us *with groanings* too deep for words." He can even be *lied to* (Acts 5:3), and can *"forbid"* (Acts 16:6).

The word "spirit" has several meanings in its New Testament usage and the particular meaning in a passage must be determined from the context. It can mean *the human spirit* (Acts 7:50); *attitude of mind* (John 4:24); *angels* (Heb. 1:14); *unclean spirits* (Mark 5:13); spirit of faith (2 Cor. 4:13); spirit of gentleness (1 Cor. 4:21); spirit of timidity (2 Tim. 1:7); spirit of error (1 John 4:6); spirit of the world (1 Cor. 2:12); and many other meanings, including that of the Holy Spirit Himself as indicated above. The adjective *Holy* does not necessarily need to be present for the term to designate the third person of the Godhead, as in 1 Cor. 2:10, "God has revealed to us through the Spirit." He is also called the Spirit of God (1 Cor. 2:11), the Spirit of Christ (1 Pet. 1:11), and other designations as well. The context in every case must aid in distinguishing and sharpening the specific meaning of the particular usage.

Expressions in NT Times

The New Testament mentions several varying influences of the Holy Spirit upon men in New Testament times (some of which are also influences on us today) and these can be classified in at least five different expressions:

1. The *baptism* of the Holy Spirit (Acts 2:1-4; 10:44-47; 11:15,16). This measure or influence was used on only two occasions in the NT, at Pentecost for the apostles and at the house of Cornelius (Acts 11:17) to show divine approval of Gentile admission into the Christian fold. Characteristics of this manifestation of the Spirit are that its coming was *visible* ("tongues as of fire") and *audible* ("rushing wind") and thus this influence was knowable to all bystanders through their own eyes and ears.

Such a manifestation is unknown in modern times and all claims of such fall short of having these visible and audible distinguishing characteristics. Therefore the "baptism" of the Holy Spirit should not be considered as available today.

2. The *miraculous gifts* (1 Cor. 12:1-11; 14:1-18; Acts 8:14-18; Rom. 12:6-8; Mark 16:20). These signs or powers were special abilities conferred upon certain Christians in the early chruch for purposes of preaching and of

3

"confirming the word" and thus enabling them to carry on the Lord's work effectively *before* the word was completed in written form in the several NT books.

These miraculous gifts "passed away" (1 Cor. 13:8-10; Eph. 4:11-13) when "that which is perfect" (the completed NT) came (about the close of the first century A.D.), since they were no longer needed for the purposes for which such gifts were given.

3. The *inspired word* (1 Cor. 2:12, 13; 2 Cor. 3:3; Acts 2:4; James 1:21; Rom. 1:17; 10:17). This is the inspired (Spirit guided and controlled) gospel message — the teaching of Christ which was spoken orally by inspired men in the first century and was written down in the NT by inspiration and thus is still the power of God and His word unto salvation to all future generations (Rom. 1:16). It is our only authority as a revelation of God in Christianity, and all religious knowledge known today is necessarily limited to what the inspired written word teaches.

4. The *indwelling Spirit* (John 7:38, 39; 14; 17; Acts 2:38; 5:32; 1 Cor. 6:19; Gal. 4:6; Eph. 1:13; 4:30; 2 Tim. 1:14; James 4:5). This manifestation (of the personal Holy Spirit dwelling in the body of the Christian) is also available to Christians today, but is only available to children of God ("because you are sons") and is not available to alien sinners. It will be shown later that this expression is the possession of *today's* Christian. Here we simply observe that if a personal demon or evil spirit can dwell in the body of a living human (as in Mark 1:23-26; 5:2-17), the personal Holy Spirit can obviously also do so. Indeed the presence of the Spirit in us is the seal of our sonship and redemption (Eph. 1:13; 4:30) and is a gift to us from the Father as a pledge (down-payment) or earnest of our future inheritance (2 Cor. 1:22; 5:5).

We should note that the NT passages cited here for the indwelling Spirit cannot be satisfactorily explained in meaning by either manifestation of the first three categories. To attempt to substitute the terms "baptism," "miraculous gifts," or "inspired word" for "Spirit" in the passages under point 4 is to see that the fourth category of the indwelling Spirit is both logical and needed.

5. As a *providential help.* This expression is also an activity of today. The fact of *God's* providential activity is abundantly taught in the NT (e.g., Rom. 8:28 "God causes all things to work together for good..."). Since the Holy Spirit is used by the Father in some instances of His *providential* activity, we also need this "providence" classification—covering ways that the Spirit influences men and has to do with their lives providentially. For instance, the Spirit was providentially active in getting the preacher and the Ethiopian eunuch together and separated again (Acts 8:29,39), and He was providentially active with respect to getting the gospel preached to Cornelius (Acts 10:19,20; 11:12). In such instances the Spirit worked "behind the scenes" or "providentially" in behalf of the prospective convert, but *taught him* only through the inspired word. He received no *revelation* except through the word.

Review Questions

Chapter 1

1. Why cannot views about the person and work of the Holy Spirit be accepted unless they are specifically taught in the New Testament?

2. What is meant by the statement, "The Holy Spirit is a person?

3. Mention some uses of the word "spirit" in the New Testament where a person is not meant. How can this be determined?

4. List the five manifestations or expressions of the impact of the Holy Spirit upon Christians during the Christian Age. Justify each in the New Testament.

5. Which of the five manifestations of question 4 are still valid today? Why not each of the others?

Chapter 2

SOME INTERPRETATION THEORIES

In the first chapter we listed five expressions of the Spirit to men in New Testament times—baptism, miraculous gifts, the inspired word, the indwelling, and providence. (The latter two are also available today). We now list some questionable theories of interpretation concerning the influence of the Spirit in the present day.

Baptism of the Spirit—claimed by some groups as a special expression, while by others as a general one (received by every saved person). These people are no doubt sincere but are highly involved emotionally and "feel" that the doctrine is true from some experience they have rather than from any clear teaching of the New Testament.

The purposes of Holy Spirit baptism to "begin" the church and to initially empower the apostles on Pentecost, and to clarify the spiritual status of the Gentiles at the home of Cornelius, have now all been accomplished and so there is no similar need for such an unusual manifestation today. We are certain that claimed experiences of "the baptism" today are not the real baptism of the Holy Spirit of New Testament times, however, since they are not accompanied by the *visible* "tongues as of fire" or the *audible* sound as of "a rushing wind."

Miraculous Gifts (especially talking in tongues). As we

noted in the first chapter, the purpose of miraculous gifts was to "confirm the word" (Mark 16:20 and Heb. 2:1-4), by authenticating the person as God's agent. There was no New Testament then with which to compare a man's teaching, so a way was needed to distinguish false teachers from those who taught truth.

The New Testament today, however, serves as its own confirmation, and present-day teachings can be compared with the written word to "see whether they are so" and thus the original need for confirmation is now cared for without the miraculous. We note further that first century powers such as raising the dead are not even claimed — so why other miraculous gifts? Even in the first century healings were not done for mere personal gain (Timothy was urged to "take a little wine for his stomach's sake"—1 Tim. 5:23, whereas modern "faith healing" theory would no doubt have him seek supernatural aid rather than natural) but to authenticate the speaker as a true man of God who had been given the authoritative word of salvation.

Direct Operation in the conversion of an alien sinner. This modern concept, held by many, basically comes from Augustine (died 430 A.D.) but in a strong sense is also to be credited to John Calvin of the Reformation period who embellished and enhanced it somewhat. It holds that man is hereditarily totally depraved and is powerless to take even a first step in the direction of his own salvation until he is personally singled out and acted upon in a direct and immediate way by the Holy Spirit. This direct operation "saves" the individual but also is that which makes him to be an intellectual believer. The basic doctrine is that it is direct and immediate and really does not need the written or inspired word; however, this point has proved a problem—for instance, between some who hold it as a radical view and others of their own brethren who realize that the Holy Spirit doesn't make any members of their denomination where their preachers have not gone. Thus these latter now realize that preaching somehow makes a definite contribution.

None of this "direct operation" doctrine is taught in the New Testament. Faith is not based upon any power other than the word of the gospel (Romans 1:16; 10:17). No divine power of any kind ever "forces faith" in an irresistible way. In New Testament teaching faith is produced by the power resident in the preached (or taught) gospel message (Rom. 1:16; 10:17), and is accepted and appropriated by the alien sinner after being rationally and logically convicted (convinced) of the divinity and Lordship of Jesus Christ through the testimony and power of the word itself. No coercion is used upon the sinner other than the power resident in the word of the New Testament gospel message itself.

"Illumination" by the Spirit. Further probing by certain Calvinistic followers (as noted above) concerning the need for an *active* word (with at least some power) has called forth the doctrine of "Illumination," in which the Holy Spirit is considered to work *with* the word, and "illumines the word" in the mind of the reader or hearer so that we can understand it. The word alone, according to these people, without this direct and immediate illumination is powerless and inert.[1] In this view the personal Spirit is still the real power but it uses the word to supply information. Thus the doctrine is still a heavy Calvinism, but makes at least a minimal concession to the place of the gospel message in conversion. This newer view is held particularly by the more modern and the more intellectually-inclined of these particular denominationalists who have come to recognize the futility of a "Spirit alone" approach. It still does not square with the New Testament, however. It does not allow the word to be the real "seed" of the kingdom

---

[1] Ramm, Bernard, *The Pattern of Authority,* Grand Rapids: Eerdmans 1957, pp. 62,104.

(Luke 8:5-15) or to have true "begetting" power (1 Cor. 4:15) on its own. It requires the inspired word to be "inspired" a second time before it can function powerfully and produce the needed results. It still calls for the Calvinistic doctrine of predestination and election in that the Spirit has all the initiative and the convert is "depraved and helpless" and has neither freedom nor power of choice about his own salvation until the Spirit selects him and acts upon him. The influence of the word is totally nil in this view without this extra, direct illumining action of the Spirit.

In later chapters we may briefly refer to these questionable concepts about the work of the Spirit, but primarily we will be striving to make clear the New Testament's own teaching. In contemplating the whole landscape, however, it is well to be aware of these erroneous concepts.

Review   Questions

Chapter   2

1. Show why claims that "Holy Spirit baptism" as found in the early days of Christianity are not valid for today.

2. What purpose did the miraculous gifts of the first century serve?

3. How were such gifts conferred, and upon whom?

4. When did miracles cease, and what evidence is there to prove this? (See also chapter 9.)

5. What is meant by the expression, "Direct operation of the Holy Spirit in the conversion of an alien sinner?"

6. How does the New Testament say that faith comes?

7. Describe the "illumination" doctrine. What is basically wrong with it?

Chapter 3

THE SPIRIT AND THE ALIEN SINNER

We insist that the only power used to produce faith in the alien sinner is applied through the word of God. Although some are slow to see this (perhaps due to inherited Calvinism), the teaching of the New Testament is very clear about the place of the gospel in producing faith. Rom. 1:16 observes that "the gospel is power unto salvation," and Rom. 10:17 specifically states that "Faith comes from hearing, and hearing by the word (message— English Revised Version) of Christ."

That the faith-creating power for the non-Christian must necessarily be through the word is clear from the nature of faith itself. Faith is a response to testimony (intellectual impact) and must necessarily include some knowledge. To think of a faith without any factual "knowledge-content" is unthinkable. Religious truths which we accept must be intelligible and statable in a propositional statement. Any faith involves the acceptance of an idea or the affirmation of a cognition, and this is where faith begins. Biblical faith is based upon the acceptance of the propositional statements in the Bible concerning the Christ, his nature and work and other matters related to Him. To think of the Spirit producing faith, without any cognitive revelation whatever, is thus preposterous on its face, not to mention that it would be completely unbiblical and in direct opposition to clear teaching of many passages about the word, its nature, function and power (See Rom. 1:17; 10:13-17; Jas. 1:21;

Luke 8:11; 1 Cor. 2:13; 4:15). These and other passages make it clear that the word furnishes all the needed knowledge and facts on which faith can be structured. Furthermore, the word's exclusiveness in this function is indicated in that no other power for this purpose is mentioned, and passages such as 2 Cor. 4:7 point out that the treasure (saving power of the word) is in earthly (not heavenly) vessels (taught by men, not angels), and the Great Commission (Matt. 28:18-20; Mark 16:15, 16) lays it on the line about Christians getting the gospel preached that souls may be saved.

We noted in an earlier chapter that the Holy Spirit acted providentially in connection with the conversion of aliens in addition to the power and activity of the word (Acts 8; 10; 11). This was in the cases of the eunuch and of Cornelius. This providential activity, however, was no more than that and did not furnish to the prospective convert any revelatory information whatever. It did not replace the word which still had to be preached in each case in order to convey the needed revelation of God's will.

A clear distinction as to what the Spirit does through the word and separate from it is this. *Revelation* comes only through the word; *Providential Activity* of God (or of the Spirit) may occur in addition to the influence of the word. "Revelation" here is defined as that which provides a communication from God's mind to man's mind of religious knowledge —cognitive information; factual or historical statements; instructions; commands and promises. All of such *revelation* comes to the alien sinner only through the inspired word —that is its place and purpose. No man, alien sinner or Christian, during the Christian dispensation (after the completion of the NT and after the age of miracles) has received any *revelation* except through the word, according to the teaching of the NT. "Providential activity" as used here is defined as any and all activity which is in itself *non-*

14

revelational. It may make possible the contact of preacher and sinner or be otherwise incidental to the revelation of the word, but providence never provides revelation or the communication of any type message from the mind of God. This division of all divine activity today into *revelation* and *providential* (mutually exclusive) is really the key to much of the confusion of today. There is no present-day revelation (communication of a divine message) but there can well be much providential activity.

The idea from 1 Pet. 3:1-4 that a chaste wife may win her husband "without a word" must not be understood to mean that she can bring him to full faith without anyone ever saying a single word of the gospel message. It simply means that the example of her own faith will exercise "a pulling power" and cause him to be willing to investigate and accept teaching later. It also means that she should not try to win him by "nagging" (if her words produce a bad reaction) but by being a beautiful example. "Sermons seen" are said to be better than "sermons heard," but they actually only complement them — never replace them. No man can become a Christian without a knowledge of the basic facts and teaching of the gospel message as revealed in the words of the NT and a wholehearted acceptance of them.

Review Questions

Chapter 3

1. Comment on the concept that "Faith must have an intellectual content."

2. What do you think of the statement "Faith is a response to ideas that have been presented?"

3. Relate the Great Commission (Matt. 28:18-20; Mark 16:15,16) to the creation of faith.

4. Discuss the cases of the eunuch (Acts 8:29,39) and Cornelius (Acts 10:19,20; 11:12) as the Holy Spirit acting *providentially*, while the preaching of the word was still necessary for conversion.

5. Distinguish between *Revelation* and *Providential Activity*. Is either one used today?

6. Can God use the Holy Spirit in His Providential Activity today? (See Hebrews 1:13,14).

7. What is the true understanding of the 1 Peter 3:1-4 passage?

Chapter 4

THE SPIRIT'S RELATION TO THE WRITTEN WORD

The inspired (written) word of the New Testament gospel message is "the sword of the Spirit" (Eph. 6:17; Heb. 4:12). It is a powerful sword in a spiritual way, even to the ability to change a hardened, calloused sinner into a godly saint. The word is "the power of God unto salvation" (Rom. 1:16); faith is produced by it (Rom. 10:17); it is "able to save souls" (James 1:21); it is the "seed of the kingdom" (Luke 8:11); through it the Holy Spirit communicates "spiritual thoughts" (1 Cor. 2:13); and Paul "begot" people spiritually "through the gospel" (1 Cor. 4:15).

This is why Christians, who have "this treasure in earthen vessels" (2 Cor. 4:7) at their disposal are obligated to preach the gospel to every creature (Matt. 28:18-20; Mark 16:15, 16). It is through preaching that disciples are made, and without the word no disciples can be made. "How then shall they call on them in whom they have not believed? And how shall they believe in Him whom they have not heard? And how shall they hear without a preacher?" (Rom. 10:14). In a way this perhaps is beyond human comprehension, the "wonderful words of life" of the gospel story can indeed bring spiritual life to the unsaved, and in God's plan, this is the only avenue through which the new life can be had. The new birth requires the "begetting" of the word by the Spirit (John 3:5,6).

17

Even though the personal Holy Spirit and His word work closely together as "sword-wielder" and sword, we must remember to keep them logically distinct from each other. The Spirit is not the word, which is His tool or power or an expression of His influence. He must not be equated with the word in NT exegesis unless there is a clear contextual justification for understanding that what is meant in the particular passage is, exclusively, the power of the word. Words have central and basic meanings, but also they may have secondary meanings, such as are found in figures of speech of different types. It is a rule of interpretation, commonly recognized, that when a term is used in a text the central and basic meaning is the one meant, unless some contextual situation or other clear teaching demands a figurative or secondary meaning. Dungan's *Hermeneutics* (p. 184) gives as his first rule for determining the meaning of words:

> "Rule 1. *All words are to be understood in their literal sense, unless the evident meaning of the context forbids.*" (His italics) — "Figures are the exception, literal language the rule; hence we are not to regard anything as figurative until we feel compelled to do so by the evident import of the passage. And even here great caution should be observed. We are very apt to regard contexts as teaching some theory which we have in our minds. And having so determined, anything to the contrary will be regarded as a mistaken interpretation; hence, if the literal meaning of the words shall be found to oppose our speculations, we are ready to give to the words in question some figurative import that will better agree with our preconceived opinions. Let us be sure that the meaning of the author has demanded that the language be regarded in a figurative sense, and that it is not our theory which has made the necessity."

In the light of this pointed, No. 1 rule for interpreting meanings, the Rom. 8:11 expression, "His Spirit who indwells you" means that the literal, personal Holy Spirit Himself dwells in the Christian, unless "the evident meaning of the context forbids" and in this case it does not. The literal meaning of the expression "Holy Spirit" is the *Holy Spirit*, the personal third member of the Godhead and not a figurative, secondary or remote meaning such as an influence or other expression of the power of the Spirit (nor is it His sword).

It is arbitrary and irresponsible exegesis to declare that the *mode* or *manner* of indwelling is not indicated in Rom. 8:11. When it says "The Holy Spirit in us" *it means the personal Holy Spirit*, for that is the *literal* meaning of the term. For any other meaning to obtain, the interpreter must show that "the evident meaning of the context forbids."

The relation of the Spirit and the Christian will be discussed later, but here we simply note the interpretative rule that demands the basic and central meaning for any expression unless another meaning is clearly demanded. It is not as if each possible meaning had an equal chance at being the meaning intended in a given text — the basic meaning is always the correct one, automatically, until proven otherwise!

A clear distinction between the word and the Spirit is noticeable in such passages as 1 Thess. 1:5, "for our gospel did not come by you *in word only, but also in power and in the Holy Spirit*, with full conviction," and Heb. 6:4,5, "For in the case of those who have been once enlightened and have tasted of the heavenly gift and have been made *partakers of the Holy Spirit*, and have *tasted the good word* of God and the power sof the age to come." In many instances where the term "Holy Spirit" is used in the NT it obviously means the personal Holy Spirit Himself. This must, therefore, be the first choice in interpretation where the term occurs. This means that we should be careful not to jump to the conclusion that when the term is found in the NT it means only "the teaching influence of the inspired word." The latter is a correct conclusion only when clearly *demanded* by contextual or other considerations — otherwise it means the personal Spirit.

The citing of John 6:63 ("It is the Spirit who gives life; the flesh profits nothing; the words that I have spoken to you are spirit and are life") does not mean that the word and the Holy Spirit are equated, or that "word" can be substituted for "Spirit." It simply points out that Jesus' words lead and guide into the spiritual life and thus cooperate with and are used (as a sword) by the Holy Spirit for this purpose.

The word produces spiritual life and is conducive to its upbuilding in the Christian. The word of the gospel is basic to revelation, and is powerful and completely adequate to us for this purpose. All that we know about the Spirit and His activity comes to us through the word, but we, of course, should not attribute to the word all the power and influence that belongs to the Spirit Himself because there are some powers and activities which Biblical teaching indicates is reserved to the personal Spirit Himself.

It is true that many (not all) of the activities of the Holy Spirit described in the NT are also described as activities of the word of God. Instances of this are well known and are too numerous to call for space here. All agree that this is so. What is not agreed by all, however, is that identical operation and influence of the Spirit and the word in some ways and in some situations makes them to be "logically identical" themselves, or allows *word* to be substituted for *Spirit* in a given passage with any degree of arbitrariness. The Spirit and His sword both accomplish many of the same things — just as a soldier and his sword may both act in the killing of a man. But this does not imply that the soldier and the sword are identically the same thing, neither does it mean that the soldier is limited to the use of the sword in all that he may do. The Spirit and the word, working conjointly, do many things. But the Spirit is not the word and is not limited to the use of the written word in all that He does, for instance, *help our weaknesses,* or *intercede*—Rom. 8:26—"the Spirit also helps our weaknesses; for we know not how to pray as we should, but the Spirit Himself intercedes for us with groanings too deep for words."

For us to come to a greater knowledge about the influence of the personal Spirit, however, does not mean that we depreciate the word and its power. We must remain open minded to be able to receive and accept all the New Testament's teaching on this or any other 'subject. The word is the final answer on any point.

For Christ and the Spirit to have common functions does not argue for their identity, nor does it argue for each to be limited in His doings to the same things that are performed by the other. They can have exclusive functions as well as common ones. So also, Christ and the Father share in many functions and ministries in behalf of Christians, yet they are distinct persons and each does some things for Christians that the other does not do. For these reasons also we must be careful about loosely equating the Spirit and the word, or deciding that when we find "Spirit" in a text it exclusively means "the teaching influence of the Spirit through the written word." If it should mean the latter it will be for a clearly discernible reason.

Sometimes Eph. 5:18 ("And be not drunken with wine, wherein is riot, but *be filled with the Spirit;* speaking to one another in psalms, and hymns, and spiritual songs . . .") and Col. 3:16 (*"Let the word of Christ dwell in you richly;* in all wisdom teaching and admonishing one another with psalms and hymns and spiritual songs, singing with grace . . .") are considered to be *completely* parallel, in that since both have the phrases about "psalms and hymns and spiritual songs" — the phrases "filled with the Spirit" and "word dwell in you richly" are identical in meaning — that is, they are only different ways of saying exactly the same thing — and

21

thus, the only *way one is filled with the Spirit is through the influence of the word!* This is unsound reasoning.

It is true that much material in Ephesians and Colossians is generally parallel — but it does not follow that these two phrases mean the same thing — it could be that the Spirit intended to say both things.

If "be filled with the Spirit" means "let the word dwell richly," then we have a peculiar statement in Luke 1:41 where Elizabeth was "filled with the Spirit" at the moment the baby "leaped in her womb" when she heard Mary's greeting. Does this mean that "the word dwelt richly" within Elizabeth at the instant the baby leaped?

In Acts 2:4 the apostles were "filled with the Spirit" and "began to speak with other tongues," at the time of their baptism with the Holy Spirit on Pentecost, but surely this means more than "the word dwelt in them richly" in the same sense that it dwells in us. If being "filled with the Spirit" in Eph. 5:19 means exactly "Let the word dwell in you richly" in Col. 3:16, then these other expressions of "being filled with the Spirit" (of Luke 1:41 and Acts 2:4) also might mean "Let the word dwell in you richly." This, then, reduces the argument of their being identical and "the only way one is filled with the Spirit is through the influence of the word" to absurdity.

The word is powerful and so is the Holy Spirit. They are not identical either in nature or function and the terms are not automatically interchangeable, even though they work conjointly and many things done by one can also be said of the other.

Review Questions

Chapter 4

1. Compare the word to a seed.

2. In the figure of the new birth what is the place of the word? Of the Spirit?

3. In your own thoughts, how can a message carry such spiritual power?

4. What is Dungan's "first rule" of interpretation? How does it apply to Romans 8:11?

5. Distinguish between the Spirit and the word. What is the function of each? Why must they be kept logically distinct?

6. Comment on the Father, Son and Holy Spirit being "three in one" as to personhood, yet each having some differing functions.

Chapter 5

THE SPIRIT AND THE CHRISTIAN

There are uncounted blessings that come to Christians through the word. Christians receive teaching influence from God's *word-revelation* just the same as do alien sinners. There is much *teaching*—all truth—(leading to full spiritual maturity) that the Christian needs and the word is able to supply. Indeed all revelation to the Christian (as well as to the alien) comes through the word. The Christian knows no facts, has no information about God—of His plans or purposes—indeed, no religious knowledge at all except on the basis of having learned it through the word. The denominational concept of *"knowing* you are saved" by a *feeling* that is "better felt than told" is a subjectivity that is non-verifiable in any way (not even by New Testament teaching), and, therefore, a concept which one could easily be mistaken about. Knowledge that comes through the New Testament, however, is objective, definite, for all alike, and publicly knowable.

Edification and spiritual development of the Christian are based upon his "growth in knowledge" (2 Pet. 3:18). This knowledge comes through the word and its influence in his life. Such knowledge is a fruit of the *revelatory* activity of God through His word, and is thus distinct from any providential or other activity of the personal Spirit.

Providence and the Christian

In considering all of the Spirit's possible influences on the Christian, we have to think of the areas of both *revelation* and *providence* and analyze them as fully as we can. In this chapter, however, we discuss God's *providence*, which is a strong NT concept and is even a NT word (Heb. 11:40), though in a broad sense. The term "providence" normally means the activity that God engages in in behalf of human beings that is different from His revelation to them. In providence He works "behind the scenes" or in ways that man can never be sure of. For instance, an answer to prayer may be providential, but there is never a communication from God's mind that makes one sure that the prayer was answered. We may believe but we never can be certain that any given prayer has been answered; likewise, we may believe that God has been directing our lives providentially but there is no empirical knowledge (through any of our five senses) or certainty for us about it—only our belief. There is *no cognitive communication* whatever. God does not today communicate *messages* to people as the Holy Spirit did to Paul (Acts 16:6, 7) when He forbade him to go into Bithynia; or even give *signs* (to communicate God's favorable or unfavorable attitude about a matter) such as the incident of Gideon's fleece (Judges 6:36-40) not even any *hints* or *nudges* that might be interpreted cognitively. There is simply no objective revelation of God's mind or will today, providentially or otherwise, according to the NT.

But this is not to say that there is no activity at all on God's part. Indeed there is much of God's activity in the world today, separate from the influence of His word. This type of activity is rightly called providence. We credit it to the Father, but since we have no revelation from the word on the point, we have no idea *how* it is accomplished. We expect to later demonstrate that the Spirit is sometimes used in providence, but we insist that *never is any new revelation communicated* in such activity.

Special Providence

Providence essentially means God's interposing in man's affairs or influencing man's life in ways different from the ordinary workings of natural law and other than through the written word. "Special providence" means "for special individuals or groups" and not general. That there is such a thing as special providence taught in the NT could be established by one proof-text alone, but there are many:

1. *Prayer answered* is an example of special providence (See Matt. 7:7-11; Jas. 5:16; Jas. 1:5; 1 Peter 3:12, 13). To answer any prayer means a decision and an act of God separate from the written word. It means that things get done that would not have otherwise been accomplished—even such a thing as a Christian's "getting wisdom." (Jas. 1:5).

2. God *punishes evil people* in this life. (Rom. 12:19-13:4).

3. God consciously *blesses Christians* in this life (1 Pet. 5:5-7; 2 Cor. 9:6-11; Rom 8:28, 32). Some of these blessings are dependent upon our yielding properly, in which case God must make continuing, conscious decisions as He influences and blesses us, and makes things "work for good" for us. Certainly more is going on here than the influence upon us of the written word alone.

4. God *delivers us from temptation* (1 Cor. 10:12, 13) in that He acts *in every temptation* to "make a way of escape." He consciously keeps Satan "on a leash" and permits him to go so far in tempting each of us, but no further. Since every person is different, God is quite active in "playing by ear" His providential help in respect to temptations for individuals.

5. God *chastens His children* 1 Pet. 5:10; Heb. 12:6-10), and as the Potter and the clay, He is constantly at work moulding our lives (Rom. 9:18-21).

6. He *directs our lives* (Jer. 10:23, Jas. 4:13-15). What happens in a given individual's life is clearly dependent upon God's will.

7. God *provides* even the *material necessities* (Matt. 6: 25-33) and this is not based on general laws, but is conditioned on the degree to which we as individuals "seek first the kingdom."

All of this teaching about God's providence means that God is near us, over us, and about us constantly. It should strengthen our faith to realize that the Father is vitally and specifically interested in every one of us—He even knows the number of hairs on our heads! This should make us realize that it PAYS to be a Christian— that with all of this help from God we cannot possibly lose if we keep clinging to Him in faith. "Who is he that will harm you, if ye be zealous of that which is good?" (1 Pet. 3:13). "He careth for you" (1 Pet. 5:7).

We must discount the idea of *"biblical Deism"* (if any hold it), which assumes that "God started the Christian system and left the Bible down here to do what it could, but meanwhile He, Christ, and the Spirit have all retired to heaven and have nothing to do with the world until the end, when they will come back and check up to see how it all worked out!"

God, the Spirit, and the Bible are all very much active in the world today. The Father is not far from each one of us (Acts 17:27). Even angels are sent out to "render service" (act providentially) on behalf of Christians (Heb. 1:14). The Spirit intercedes in our behalf by rewording our prayers (Rom. 8:26). He helps us "put to death the deeds of the body" (Rom. 8:13).

It would be foolish for us to say *how* God works providentially, since we have no revelation on the point. But however He works, it is still only providence and there is no new revelation or new knowledge communicated. The fact of providence is abundantly taught and this should be believed and relied upon, but it is equally clear that the day of *revelation* ended about the close of the first century A.D. with the close of the age of miracles. Revelation "was once for all delivered" (Jude 3).

Chapter 5

1. Distinguished between subjective and objective knowledge. Which is the more certain?

2. Why can we not know whether God is acting providentially for us?

3. Discuss the concept of special providence. Give some passages that relate to this.

4. Does God go beyond "the influence of the word" in His providential activity?

5. Might the Holy Spirit be involved in providential activity? If so, why? If not, why?

6. If the Holy Spirit is *providentially* active for us, would it be through the word, or perhaps in person?

7. Is providential help conditional upon our attitude or actions?

8. What does the concept of an active providence do to our understanding about the Christian life?

9. What are the implications of a "Biblical" Deism?

Chapter 6

THE INDWELLING SPIRIT

The question of *whether* the Holy Spirit *personally indwells* Christians is a separate question from that of *how* the Spirit *influences* Christians, and may be considered independently.

In Romans 4:11 we note that Abraham's circumcision was a *sign* and a *seal* of his righteousness. In Col. 2:11, 12 we read "You were circumcised with a circumcision made without hands, in the removal of the body of the flesh by the circumcision of Christ; having been buried with Him through faith in the working of God," and we note that in the New Covenant, "spiritual circumcision" is thus closely connected with Christian baptism. Many denominationalists think that baptism itself *is* the Christian's seal, but the New Testament makes it quite clear that the *seal* of righteousness (of redemption and sonship) for the Christian is the Holy Spirit—Eph. 1:13 ("in whom, having also believed, ye were sealed with the Holy Spirit of promise which is an earnest of our inheritance"); Eph. 4:30 ("and grieve not the Holy Spirit of God, in whome ye were sealed unto the day of redemption"); and 2 Cor. 1:21, 22 ("He who establishes us with you in Christ and anointed us is God, who also sealed us and gave us the Spirit in our hearts as a pledge.")

Since Abraham's fleshly circumcision was a seal of his sonship, and since the Christian experiences a spiritual circumcision, logically it is his seal of sonship. The above

31

passages, however, declare this spiritual circumcision to be "the Holy Spirit given" to the Christian. The timing of this gift and seal is at or in baptism into Christ, since Col. 2:11,12 indicates that all who were baptized had received "the circumcision of Christ." Clearly, then, when one is baptized he receives the Spirit as a gift and as a seal and as a pledge of his future inheritance. Though the gift of the Spirit as a seal is not *chronologically* different from baptism, it is a *logically* distinct act. This fact makes clear other passages which bear on the Spirit's relation to the Christian:

In John 7:38, 39 we read, "He that believeth on me, as the scripture hath said, from within him shall flow rivers of living water. But this spake he of the Spirit, which they that believed on him were to receive: for the Spirit was not yet given; because Jesus was not yet glorified." This passage clearly indicates that with the coming of the Christian dispensation (after Jesus' glorification) there was to be a reception of the Spirit by them "that believe" which was to be different from any expression given in any former dispensation. This gift (and seal) would of course also be different from the *word* of the gospel, which must be received *before* one could believe and in order to produce the faith. One must receive the word and believe it before he can qualify to receive this special expression of the Spirit, which was inaugurated with the coming of the Christian dispensation. It was not to be limited to the apostles, since *all who believe* are to receive it.

This understanding also makes clear the expression in Acts 2:38, "and, ye shall receive the gift of the Holy Spirit." Such is promised to *every* penitent baptized believer just the same as "the remission of sins" is promised to him. (This gift is neither "the word," nor "eternal life" or "the blessings of the gospel" as some interpreters have held, in which cases the Spirit would be the giver rather than the object given.) In Acts 2:38, however, God is definitely the giver, and the Spirit is that which is given, as the following passages make clear:

John 7:39 — "the Spirit was not yet given."

2 Cor. 1:21, 22 — "God, who also sealed us and gave us the Spirit in our hearts as a pledge." (Note: God is the subject, the Spirit is the object, and the verb is "gave.")

2 Cor. 5:5 — "God, who gave to us the Spirit as a pledge." (No doubt that here the Spirit is the object given.)

1 Thess. 4:8 — "...God, who gives His Holy Spirit to you."

The gift of the Spirit to the Christian at the time he becomes a Christian serves as a seal (identification) and as an earnest (pledge or "downpayment") on our future inheritance in heaven. This gift is peculiar to the Christian, not being available for aliens, nor available during previous dispensations—John the Baptist's disciples at Ephesus (Acts 19:1-7) had to be rebaptized since they had not been taught correctly. The gift of the Spirit was not made in connection with John's baptism (though the latter was "for remission of sins"—Mark 1:4) and the gift of the Holy Spirit is thus a distinctive accompaniment of Christian baptism.

No argument denying the personal indwelling Spirit has satisfactorily explained these passages concerning the seal received by the Christian, in the knowledge of this author, and they call for explanation. No good explanation is offered for what the Christian receives *at baptism* in the sense of a "plus" or *new* expression of the Spirit. It cannot be the *word*, which had already been received. "*Word*" wouldn't make much sense if substituted for "*Spirit*" in these passages. Without doubt the Christian receives a new expression of the Spirit that the alien cannot have—indeed "the world cannot receive" Him (John 14:17), although it can receive the word. (The argument that "world" here includes everyone except the apostles is a strange use of the word "world"; and the claim that the Spirit was promised only to the apostles personally in John 14:16, 17 does not square with the expression in verse 16—"that He may be with you forever," since the term "forever" would not apply personally to them.) "World" here means "non-Christians."

As noted in Chapter 3, "Spirit" in the above passages obviously from the context must mean the literal, personal Spirit, given as a gift (unless it obviously means otherwise, which in this case it does not).

Other passages that support, and are made clear by, the personal indwelling of the Holy Spirit in the body of the Christian are:

1 Cor. 6:19—"Your body is a temple of the Holy Spirit who is in you, whom you have from God..." Why would "body" instead of "mind" be used here if it is the word which does the indwelling?

Acts 5:32—"We are witnesses of these things, and so is the Holy Spirit, whom God has given to those who obey Him." Is it not both possible and likely that when "Holy Spirit" is used here, the "Holy Spirit" is meant?

Gal. 4:6—"because you are Sons, God has sent forth the Spirit of His Son into our hearts, crying Abba! Father!" It is the Spirit who does the crying here (not our hearts). We know this because the Greek participle "crying" (*kradzon*) is singular in number, and *necessarily* has "Spirit" as its subject. The Greek language is definite and exact in such matters. The *word* "in our hearts" could not possibly "cry," "Abba! Father!" Only a person can do that!

In reply to those who interpret *Spirit* of Gal. 4:6 to mean only the "disposition" of His Son, we ask how can a *disposition* cry "Abba! Father!"? (Remember that the Greek of the text *demands* that the Spirit in this verse is the one who does the crying!)

The impact of this one point alone (the Spirit's crying from within us) makes it sure that the manifestation of the Spirit which indwells Christians is the personal Spirit Himself. This alone should convince us as to the *how* of the indwelling!

2 Tim. 1:14—"Guard through the Holy Spirit who dwells in us, the treasure which has been entrusted to you." Timothy was to use the agency of the indwelling Spirit to guard the treasure (thing entrusted), which deposit is apparently the message of truth (or word of God) as 1 Tim. 6:20 also implies. If this be true, the indwelling Spirit is *not the word* but is to be used to *guard the word* of truth from being contaminated.

James 4:5 (NASB margin)—"The Spirit which He has made to dwell in us jealously desires us." The personal characteristic is obvious here.

To accept the fact of the personal indwelling of the Spirit and that of providential activity separate from the teaching influence of the word does not mean that one accepts any revelatory activity today. There is no *baptism* of the Spirit, no miraculous gift, no "direct operation in conversion," no new revelation or communication of any type of knowledge. It simply means to accept the NT teaching of the *fact* of the personal Spirit with whatever help and advantages He provides. The fact of personal indwelling of the Holy Spirit in a Christian's body is no more illogical than for demons or evil spirits to dwell in a human body (See Luke 7:21; 8:2; Acts 19:12). Neither does it call for a new *incarnation* of Divinity (as Christ became incarnate) any more than demon possession in NT days incarnated Satan. The human spirit is not changed in nature in either case. It simply means that the human spirit has a guest, either welcome or unwelcome—in the case of Holy Spirit residing in us, or a demon in the case of certain New Testament characters. Neither does this involve a "fragmentation" of the Holy Spirit into small segments. If God the Father can be omnipresent, so also can the Holy Spirit.

Not only is there no new revelation through the fact of the indwelling Spirit, but there is no way to be certain of His presence, except through faith in the word which teaches the fact of the indwelling. There are no "spine tingles" or any other type of sensual experience. This would change faith into knowledge, and change Christianity into a different type of religion entirely. We know that He indwells us personally just as we know we have remission of sins. It is dependence upon the teaching of the word that gives us the assurance in each case, not a "feeling."

In summary, note that the Spirit in a new, significant and distinctive way is promised and then is given to the new Christian, at or in baptism, as a seal. The influence of the word does not fit this expression, since aliens receive the word and can be influenced by it, even if they never become Christians.

The Spirit, as the object, is given by the Father to Christians as a seal and earnest. (Acts 5:32; 2 Cor. 1:22, 23; 2 Cor. 5:5; Gal. 4:6). The words "Spirit" and "Holy Spirit" mean "the Holy Spirit" personally, unless there is a definite and clear indication otherwise in any context.

The word "crying" (Gk. *kradzon*) in Gal. 4:6 can refer only to the Spirit, and only persons could cry "Abba! Father!" The Spirit is "in our hearts" at the time of such crying, according to the passage. This point is objective proof of the personal indwelling of the Spirit. No opposing interpretation is possible.

Numerous other passages ring clear and true when the personal indwelling is accepted. This does not mean any new revelation, however; nor does it mean "direct operation," present-day miracles or baptism of the Spirit.

Chapter 6

1. Define: seal; earnest; pledge. What does the New Testament say these are?

2. In the light of passages referred to in this chapter is the Holy Spirit the "object given" or the subject, who does the giving?

3. When is the gift of the Spirit given and received? How does this time element relate to one's reception of the teaching influence of the word?

4. Comment on the Christian's receiving something *new* to him at his baptism, and which is called the gift of the Holy Spirit. Had he obtained any teaching influence of the word *before* he became a Christian?

5. Why does faith that the Spirit personally dwells within us *not* require that we: Become inspired; become able to "speak in tongues"; or work miracles, as some gifts in the first century allowed?

6. What is the force of the Spirit's crying from within us as we note in Gal. 4:6?

Chapter 7

THE SIGNIFICANCE
OF THE INDWELLING

We believe that we have established without question the fact of the personal indwelling of the Holy Spirit in the Christian, in the light of NT teaching. Major points leading to this are: He is to be "given" as a seal and an earnest to every new Christian; this "plus" manifestation is obviously not "the influence of the word," which is received by alien sinners before they can become Christians; many passages state that the Holy Spirit dwells in the Christian, and the first rule of the meaning of words demands that this be the literal, personal Holy Spirit, since there is no clear evidence to the contrary; in Gal. 4:6 we are told that "God has sent forth the Spirit of His Son into our hearts, crying Abba! Father!" and the Greek language (the participle *kradzon*) makes it definite that it is the Spirit who does the "crying" "within our hearts" (No other interpretation is possible here, and there is no textual variant to raise any possible alternative application.)—only a person can cry, "Father, Father;" and the personal Spirit who is doing the crying is "in our hearts" at the time of the crying.

To realize that the Spirit dwells *personally* in us, without question, will call for some of us to have another look at many passages that we have been interpreting in another way, but really they will be clearer and more meaningful than before. We point out, however, that the fact of the personal indwelling of the Spirit does NOT

39

mean several things—some of which have been asserted about the views of those who accept the personal indwelling.

The fact of the personal indwelling does *not* mean that any of the erroneous interpretative theories about the Holy Spirit discussed in Chapter 2 are true. It does *not* imply that there is a present-day baptism of the Spirit, nor present-day miracles, direct operation of the Spirit in conversion, or tongue-speaking. Some interpreters, without thinking these concepts through to a clear and logical conclusion, assume that to believe in the personal indwelling logically opens one up to believing in one or more of these denominational doctrines. Such interpreters simply ought to analyze the categories more clearly and they will be seen to have no necessary or logical relation. Once I heard an anti-Sunday-School preacher argue that to accept classes as scriptural would mean that you would have a musical instrument as the next step, and that the logic allowing the one would also allow the other. Such interpreters simply need to study the issues out more thoroughly.

As evil spirits in NT days could enter and dwell in a human body as an "unwanted guest" of the man, the Holy Spirit can also inhabit a human body (as a welcome guest), but in each instance there is no reason to understand that the guest Spirit will force decisions of the man separate from his own will or communicate new information to him in the sense of revelation. There is no reason to assume that the indwelling Spirit will work miracles in this capacity. He actually works only providentially (non-revelationally), so far as the NT teaches, though His position may enable Him to be more helpful in a providential way. Apparently evil spirits dwelling in people had some advantage in making trouble for the individual by reason of dwelling inside his body.

How does one *know* that the Spirit dwells in his body? The answer is *by faith!* This is the only way anyone can know anything relative to Christianity. We know we are children of God by faith. We know and have confidence in our remission of sins by faith. All this comes through the teaching of the word. There are no empirical (five-senses) manifestations, such as a tingling of the spine or a palpitation of the heart. "We walk by faith and not by sight" (2 Cor. 5:7) in this as well as in all other matters of Christianity. If there were any empirical or objective evidence of any kind, Christianity would no longer be a faith religion. There is simply no other way of knowing, but faith is adequate to the need when we have the proper understanding of the teaching of the word on any point. When Paul (Acts 19:2) asked the converts at Ephesus about their having received the Spirit, their negative reply was not based upon any sensation or empirical knowledge, but upon their faulty teaching with respect to the matter. John's baptism was unaccompanied by the gift of the Spirit, and they had received teaching only concerning his baptism, thus they then had to have Christian baptism. Their reception of the Spirit, about which he inquired, was the gift of the Spirit as a seal and earnest, which all Christians receive. Any question to them about miraculous gifts would not have been in point, since not all Christians received miraculous gifts. The fact that Paul went ahead and conferred miraculous gifts upon them after they were baptized into Christ and had received the gift of the Spirit was normal in such an early Christian community, but since they were not truly Christian without Christian baptism and the gift of the Spirit, he checked on this matter to determine their eligibility for miraculous gifts before attempting to confer them through laying on of his hands.

In this connection, there is no empirical or objective way for *other people* to determine by one's Spiritual fruit (Gal. 5:22) whether or not one is truly a Christian. The true Christian will produce true spiritual fruit, just as he will have some of his prayers answered. But non-Christians may do *some* good deeds, just as they also may (coincidentally) have blessings for which they have prayed. (These would not be "fruit of the Spirit" in such a case, however.) Faith, rather than clear cut empirical proof, is how we know in either case whether one is a Christian, but the real Christian will bear the fruit of the Spirit to some degree.

How God and Christ Dwell in Us

Both the Father (1 John 4:15) and Christ (Col. 1:27; Eph. 3:17) dwell in the Christian. The problem is raised as to how they dwell in us. Some say that they dwell in us only in the same manner as the Spirit, which they assume to be only through the influence of the word in our lives. IT IS TRUE that all three members of the Godhead dwell in us in a sense through the teaching influence of the word, and this is no small matter. The teachings of *Christ* are a powerful influence in our lives, but they were imparted by the *Spirit*, and authorized by the *Father*, so when the influence of the word exists in our lives, there is no doubt but that in a real sense each member of the Godhead dwells in us in this manner. There is no reason to think, however, that Deity dwells in Christians exclusively through the word; nothing in the Bible indicates this. In fact it has been shown in previous chapters that the Spirit literally and personally dwells in Christians. Inasmuch as the Father, the Son, and the Spirit are in truth one, then in whatever one does, He represents the others, and logically, therefore, when the Spirit literally dwells in Christians, as is overwhelmingly indicated, both the Father and the Son also dwell in them in a representative sense. This sense adequately explains the passages which state that God and Christ dwell in us, which are not adequately explained by the concept of their dwelling in us through the word. It is nowhere taught that the Father and the Son dwell in us *in the same way* that it is taught that

42

the Spirit dwells in us. We do not have the clear and abundant references about their being in us as we do of His. Romans 8:9-11 illustrates the point.

An argument based on Gal. 3:2 is made to deny personal indwelling of the Spirit in favor of its being only through the word—"Did ye receive the Spirit *out of* (Gk. *ek*) the works of the law or *out of* the hearing of faith," in which case it is emphasized that "the Spirit is received through the *hearing* process." The truth of the matter is that Paul is contrasting the entire legal system of Moses with the Christian system, which is a non-legal system. As a point in his argument, of discounting the present validity of the law, he simply reminds them that the Spirit was not given under the legal system but is under the Christian system. It is not contextually justifiable to make out of this a detailed blue-print of *how* the Spirit is given.

A very important passage is found in Eph. 3:16-19, where it is indicated that Christ may dwell in our hearts "through faith." Since faith is dependent upon the word (Rom. 10:17), the *only way* Christ can dwell in us is said to be *through the word*. And if Christ, so also the Spirit and the Father. This argument obviously seems rather oversimplified, but indeed, it can be true up to a point. One thing wrong, however, is that there is nothing here to indicate that this is *the only, the exclusive*, way that Deity can dwell in humanity, which is the *necessary* conclusion to those who hold this point of view. Again, it *is* through faith in the teaching of the word that we understand that the Spirit dwells personally within us. The knowledge is part of the faith system. So it begs the question to find in this passage the doctrine of Spirit indwelling through *the word only*.

Again, *the word does dwell in us*, and all members of the Godhead do truly dwell in us *through the word*. This understanding helps to explain *some* passages of scripture; but none of them, however, teach that Deity dwells in Christians *only* and exclusively through the word. This is an assumed conclusion which finds no Biblical support. Some teachings of the NT reveal clearly the personal indwelling of the Spirit, and others are made clearer by this understanding. In no case, however, does this involve erroneous teachings, such as present-day Spirit baptism, tongues, miracles, or direct operation in conversion.

Review   Questions

Chapter   7

1. What new understandings about the nature of the Christian religion come to us when we realize the possibility of the personal indwelling?

2. What does the fact of the personal indwelling NOT mean?

3. How do Christians get valid religious knowledge? Should it come through sense-experiences? Why?

4. Discuss the case of the Ephesian converts (Acts 19:1-6) both as to the reception of the Spirit and as to their receiving some miraculous gifts.

5. What about God and Christ dwelling in us *representatively* through the Spirit?

6. How did those who believe in "word only" indwelling of the Spirit come to decide that this is the *only* and *exclusive* way that the Spirit can dwell in Christians?

Chapter 8

THE LEADING OF THE SPIRIT

No one questions that Christians are led by the Spirit (Rom. 8:14). The problem is how? In previous lessons we have noted that He influences people both through revelation and through providential activity—all of us believe in a considerable amount of providence, even though we may individually be weak in faith with respect to it and may not lean upon it very heavily. Also all Christians believe strongly that the Holy Spirit influences Christians through the word. The real point of difference, other than the problem of the personal indwelling, is whether the Spirit *today* influences Christians in a revelatory way, other than through the word.

Those who argue "word only" have no objection to providence, but they are afraid that the others are believing in "revelation today," other than through the Bible. On the other hand, most of those who oppose the "word only" view today feel that the word-only exponents are really denying providence, when they argue that "the Spirit *influences* Christians today only through the word." It thus boils down to semantic difficulties, with arguments made vehemently, but which do not use precise enough terminology to pin-point the issues. Actually there is not as much difference between these views as some think. Yet it is true that there is the difference over the nature of the indwelling, whether personal or through the word; and we have learned of some Christians who feel that they have received definite "signals" or communications (revelation) (which are then statable in logical statements) from the Holy Spirit, in mystical experiences or peculiar "leadings" that are different from the influence of the word. This is not to deny a powerful word, in the view of this latter view, but it is definitely to claim present-day revelation, which this author unequivocally denies.

That the Spirit as author (or inspirer) of the word *leads* Christians through the powerful teachings of the word is so obvious that no one denies this. Passages are abundant that testify to this, and for one to repudiate it he would just about have to be out of his right mind. Such "leading" through the word, however, is a public, general leading (for all men alike and on equal terms). Any special or private leading done by the Spirit to any individual or group is not done by the word since its influences are open to all men equally. Any "special leading" is, therefore, providence—but this is a "behind the scenes" influence, and is never identifiable for certain as an act of God, *neither does it communicate revelatory information* nor does it ever force human action independent of the person's deliberate choice.

To say that "the Spirit influences Christians through the word" is really to say that which is also true for aliens, as He influences them through the word in leading them to faith. This statement, taken alone at face value, also denies providence, since providence is not exercised through the word. Actually the statement is not worded correctly even for the persons who normally make it—it should read, "The Spirit gives *revelation* only through the word today, but *providential influence* is exercised separate from the word." This wording obviates the lack of precision in the other.

The two basic problems, of the personal indwelling and how the Spirit influences Christians, are in some measure interrelated. Many of those who oppose personal indwelling feel that to accept it forces them to also accept "revelatory action today," but this is not true at all. If they could first accept the fact of personal indwelling they would then be more likely to understand some of the more detailed providential influences as normal and usual. This would also simplify interpretation of certain passages. To decide that there is no personal indwelling of the Spirit will necessarily affect our interpretation of certain passages, and to learn, as we have indicated earlier that it is the Spirit Himself which indwells us and not just an influence, will lead us to see a fuller and more significant meaning in several passages of the NT, some of which we note below.

General Significance

Generally speaking every Christian receives the Spirit as a seal, and as an earnest and pledge of his future inheritance in heaven. The NT makes it clear that these are a gift, from God, and that the Spirit is the object given, not the giver. This makes clear the meaning of Acts 2:38, and the concept of the personal indwelling also opens up the possibility of a more significant meaning to the term "spirituality." The seal and the earnest are a guarantee of sonship, and are an incentive to holiness, even though our knowledge of the presence of the Spirit in us is limited to faith in the word's teaching on the point. Further, when it is believed that the Spirit has such a personal and intimate relationship with the Christian's spirit, the concept of providential activity is not as remote and it is no doubt easier to realize that God truly "works all things together for good" (Romans 8:28) to them that love Him. To believe that God hears and answers prayer—even to the granting of wisdom (James 1:5)—is easier when we believe in the closeness to us of the Godhead. It is a little hard to reconcile such a prayer as "Lord, give our preacher a happy recollection of the things he has studied to deliver to us on this occasion," to the doctrine that "the Spirit influences Christians only through the teaching knowledge imparted through the word!" We all believe that God can answer such a prayer, and none of us believe that for Him to do so the preacher would have to go and study some more; but what we should all keep in mind is that in answering such a prayer God will not impart any new factual knowledge or revelation—the help will be only of a providential type, "behind the scenes." These facts explain the problem in the way that all of us have always believed, but non-precise wording as to how the Spirit influences us leaves us confused.

Special Help (All Providential)

The Spirit's crying "Abba! Father!" from a position "in our hearts" (Gal. 4:6) is a special activity in behalf of Christians that is a different influence from that of the word. Jesus used this expression (Mark 14:36), and in Romans 8:15 we learn that Christians also make this intimate cry of "Dear Father" (or as one author has likened it, "Daddy, Daddy!"). All this intensifies our conception of a strong spiritual communion and fellowship on our part with God, Christ and the Spirit (See also 1 John 1:3), and with each other. In Rom. 8:16 we learn that the Spirit bears witness *with* our spirits, and this may be in His crying "Abba Father," with us. In such experiences Christians do not learn any new revelation (they learn about this only from the word), but there are activities of the Spirit here that are not the teaching influence of the word.

The Spirit "helps our infirmities" and "intercedes for us with groanings too deep for words" (Rom. 8:26). Some have argued that the Spirit is not the one groaning here, but it is rather the Christians; but this is a failure to understand what the language says. "With unutterable groanings" is an adverbial phrase modifying "intercedes," and the subject of the verb *intercedes* (the Spirit) is necessarily the one who is doing the groaning. To realize from Gal. 4:6 that the Spirit cries "Abba! Father!" from within our hearts may keep this Rom. 8:26 interpretation from being objectionable. In any case, however, the thing that is important for our point in this passage is that the Spirit does actually *intercede*, and this is something that He does (in a *Special* way) in connection with our prayers and *in our behalf* that is different from the teaching influence of the word. Surely, those who say "word only" have not thought this matter through nor considered all the passages involved! Verse 26 says that it is the Spirit *Himself* (intensive pronoun), not an influence of His, that does the interceding, so without question here is an action of the Spirit *Himself on behalf of Christians* that is something more than the influence of the word. We have a tremendous amount of providential help available to us, and we ought to learn about it and believe it and use it. The Spirit leads providentially in ways that are beyond our comprehension.

In Romans 8:13 we learn of help from the Spirit in "putting to death the deeds of the body." Surely it is true that the word and its teaching influence gives us spiritual strength and stamina against temptations; but in view of the fact that the Spirit personally gives us aid in living the Christian life, as already noted, surely the personal Spirit, acting providentially, also gives us help and spiritual strength and stamina though we do not know specifically how.

An especially interesting note is that from Rom. 8:11, where it reads: "if the Spirit of Him who raised Jesus from the dead dwells in you, He who raised Christ Jesus from the dead will also give life to your mortal bodies through His Spirit who indwells you." Paraphrased, this means "since God's Spirit dwells in you, God, who raised Jesus from the dead will also raise your mortal bodies in the resurrection by means of His (the same) Spirit who dwells in you!" We have seen this interpreted (to defend the "word only" view) that *the Holy Spirit* will raise our bodies by words (???)—"all that are in their tombs shall hear the voice of the Son of God, and come forth—John 5:28, 29. They shall *hear his voice* and come out of the grave. In the *resurrection* the Spirit operates through the word of Christ." In our view this is quite far-fetched and is straining a great deal to keep "the teaching influence of the word" as the *only* way the Spirit influences Christians! It misses the point in that the verse, Rom.8:11, says that *God* will do the raising (as also does John 5:21), not the Spirit; and that God will do the raising *by using the Spirit* who indwells us. The Spirit is the means of the resurrection, not the agent. *The influence of the taught word is certainly not the means!* Imagine how this would paraphrase, if "the word only" is the only way the Spirit indwells the Christian— "God will resurrect your mortal bodies through the teaching influence of His word, which dwells in you." The passage is *not* saying that corpses will decide to act in harmony with the way they have been taught by the Bible and will, therefore, come forth from the grave, with no other influence upon them whatever! It says that God will use the Holy Spirit, Himself, to give life to our dead bodies—the same power that was used to resurrect Christ's body.

In Rom. 5:5 we learn that the Spirit "pours out (diffuses throughout, thoroughly disseminates) the love of God in our hearts." This is the same Spirit that "was given to us," so it is the personal Spirit. We cannot explain how He "pours out" God's love in our hearts— but this is apparently something different from our being taught.

God providentially "makes a way of escape" for us in connection with "every temptation" (1 Cor. 10:13) that we confront, and this calls for a conscious activity on His part in our behalf, separate from the teachings of the written word. Perhaps He uses the indwelling Spirit in this connection, but at least "word only" does not explain this influence in our behalf. We know that Satan tempts us, and apparently God supplies an offsetting influence of an opposite type and thus sees that we have strength and opportunity to choose for the right.

Eph. 3:16-19 is a passage that reaches spiritual depths perhaps as well as any in the NT—

> that He would grant you, according to the riches of His glory, to be strengthened with power through His Spirit in the inner man; so that Christ may dwell in your hearts through faith; and that you, being rooted and grounded in love, may be able to comprehend with all the saints which is the breadth and length and heighth and depth, and to know the love of Christ which surpasses knowledge, and that you may be filled up to all the fullness of God.

This passage states that spiritual help and spiritual appreciation are available for the Christian beyond his rational ability to understand. When we realize that the Spirit personally dwells within us and that great providential help is available for us in many ways, we are caused to be amazed at God's power and God's ways. To be strengthened "with power by His Spirit in the inner man" sounds very much like help is available even beyond the wonderful teaching help that comes through the word—and it enables us to comprehend the love of Christ in a way that is beyond ordinary rational discernment; and the idea of being "filled up to all the fulness of God" means spiritual values even beyond our present understanding. It is one thing to be taught of God through His marvelous word. It is also great and wonderful to have fellowship and communion with the Godhead on a personal basis in His family and to receive the abundant providential help that He supplies to Christians.

Chapter 8

1. Distinguish between revelation and providence, since both are supernatural activities. Are either operative today?

2. What relation is there, if any, between the influence of the written word and God's providential actions?

3. Why, possibly, are some hesitant to accept a *personal* indwelling of the Spirit?

4. Does believing in a personal indwelling provide any incentives to holiness? Are there other serendipities?

5. Describe the intimate fellowship that the Christian has in God's family. Is this a plus, for living the Christian life?

6. Comment on the Spirit's aid to the Christian as taught in Romans 8:26. In Romans 8:13.

7. Give a fair interpretation of Romans 8:11 and of Romans 5:5.

8. Comment on God's direct help in 1 Cor. 10:13, and the Spirit's help in Eph. 3:16.

Chapter 9

THE CESSATION OF REVELATION

The purpose of the miraculous or "charismatic" gifts which were used by Christians in the first century church before the New Testament was completed was to "confirm the word" (Mark 16:20; Heb. 2:3,4). By this it is meant that the true preacher of God's word was distinguished by ordinary people from those who were false teachers and impostors, since genuine miracles and signs were worked only by God's true agents. The gifts thus enabled people to know what was the true message of God. These charismatic gifts were conferred upon individuals by the laying on of the apostles' hands (Acts 8:17,18; 19:6). When the last apostle died and the last person upon whom they had laid hands died the charismatic gifts necessarily ceased. We know of no other plan for their being conferred and/or continued. Traditionally John, the last apostle, died about 96 A.D. following the close of the writing of the *Revelation*, though probably the use of charismatic gifts had already begun to wane, since most of the NT books had been written by this time. After the NT books came into existence, they were circulated widely (see Col. 4:16) and with the completed written word alone, Christians could then "test" a teacher to "see whether these things were so" (Acts 17:11). Thus after the word was put into writing, the need for charismatic gifts lessened, since both the New Testament and the gifts served the same "confirmation" purpose. So, after all the books were completed (A.D. 96), the gifts ceased completely with the death of John and the death of all upon whom gifts had been conferred. This basic conclusion is also in harmony with the interpretation of two key passages of scripture which discuss the infancy and the maturity of the church:

> 1 Cor. 13:8-12. Love never fails; but if *there are gifts* of prophecy, they will be done away; if *there are* tongues, they will cease; if *there is* knowledge, it will be done away. For we know in part, and we prophesy in part; but when the perfect comes, the partial will be done away. When I was a child, I used to speak as a child, think as a child, reason as a child; when I became a man, I did away with childish things. For now we see in a mirror dimly, but then face to face; now I know in part, but then I shall know fully just as I also have been fully known.

The *prophecy, tongues* and *knowledge* of this passage are some of the charismatic or miraculous gifts of the early church. From this passage we know that they are to "fail," "cease," and "be done away," when "the perfect (Gk. *to teleion*) comes." The interpretation of "perfect" here is crucial. If it means *Jesus Christ,* and the coming is the second coming, this would mean that the charismatic gifts are still in vogue. Religious groups who believe in present-day miraculous activities accept *Jesus* as the interpretation of the term.

Another interpretation of "perfect," (which literally means *full-grown* or *mature*) is that it means the written word or revelation (the completed New Testament). This is the correct meaning of the word, because *to teleion* in the Greek is neuter in gender and thus could not possibly apply to Jesus Christ, which interpretation would require the masculine. The neuter could, however, refer to a body of ideas such as the written revelation or completed (mature) New Testament. In this latter case the miraculous gifts ended about the time the revelation became full-grown or mature and the church entered its maturity and "did away with childish things." The figure of childhood and maturity fits this interpretation better than for "the entire history of the world until the second coming" to be counted as "childhood," with "full-grownness" being after the judgment day when an entirely new arrangement will obtain.

Our conclusion for this interpretation is further confirmed in that verse 12 speaks of "knowing *in part*" (the childhood period, when the knowledge is supplied by the charismatic gifts) and "then I shall know *fully*" (the mature full-grown age, when the full revelation has been completed). The early period of "childhood" indicates partial revelation and knowledge, while the "manhood" by contrast means the period when the revelation and knowledge (of the same type and purpose) is full and complete, which we find in the finished New Testament. The "entire church-age on earth as the childhood, and heaven as maturity" interpretation does not square with the references here to *revelation* (of the same type and purpose), since any "new knowledge" gained after getting to heaven will not be of the same type and purpose as the gift of knowledge or the New Testament, as the complete revelation of Christ's will for persons who are living the earth life.

> Eph. 4:11-16. And He gave some as apostles, and some *as* prophets, and some *as* evangelists, and some *as* pastors and teachers, for the equipping of the saints for the work of service, to the building up of the body of Christ; until we all attain to the unity of the faith, and of the knowledge of the Son of God, to a mature man, to the measure of the stature which belongs to the fullness of Christ. As a result, we are no longer to be children, tossed here and there by waves, and carried about by every wind of doctrine, by the trickery of men, by craftiness in deceitful scheming; but speaking the truth in love, we are to grow up in all *aspects* into Him, who is the head, *even* Christ, from whom the whole body, being fitted and held together by that which every joint supplies, according to the proper working of each individual part, causes the growth of the body for the building up of itself in love.

This passage also discusses the infancy of the church *until* it grows into its *unity* (the general subject of the context) or maturity—"to the knowledge of the Son of God, to a mature man . . . ." Actually the offices listed in vs.11 were set up during the infancy of the church and some of the officers were given charismatic gifts to aid in bringing the church to its full knowledge and to the growing "up in all aspects unto Him." The attainment of full knowledge or revelation, as versus the early partial knowledge, enabled the church to come to its maturity in every aspect—"to the measure of the stature which belongs to the fullness of Christ," (which is also the conclusion from 1 Cor. 13:8-12). This is not talking about what will be after we get to heaven but about the maturing of the earthly church. Those offices mentioned in this context which depended on miraculous gifts—as apostles and prophets—were done away when the revelation became complete, while the offices that use only "natural abilities augmented by the written revelation" continue permanently.

In both the above passages there is the idea of special help during the infancy of "the body of Christ" or the church, which special help gives way to the *normal* arrangement (full knowledge or full revelation) when the church comes into its maturity. Miracles were thus to cease with the completion of the written revelation (the writing of the NT) about the close of the first century.

The testimony of the early church (found in non-canonical writings) indicates "little or no evidence for miracle-working during the first fifty years of the post-Apostolic church" according to B. B. Warfield in his *Miracles: Yesterday and Today* (p. 10). (When this work was first published in 1918, it was entitled *Counterfeit Miracles*.) Its first chapter, on "The Cessation of the Charismata" is the most thorough treatment of this topic that this writer has seen and offers rather complete documentation from the writings of the early church authors. His conclusion (p. 23) is "that the power of working miracles was not extended beyond the disciples upon whom the Apostles conferred it by the imposition of their hands." He argues at length that this conclusion fits all the facts of history and "the unobserved dying out of these gifts" (p. 24) better than any other interpretation. He further says that "They belong to revelation periods, and appear only when God is speaking to His people through accredited messengers, declaring His gracious purposes" (p. 26), and he quotes from Kuyper, "He has given to the world one organically complete revelation, adapted to all, sufficient for all, provided for all, and from this one completed revelation He requires each to draw his whole spiritual sustenance" (p. 26). This argues against any later special revelations or communications to individuals—at any time from the second century on!

Two major points are made finally by Warfield—(1) "the impossibility of believing that the gifts were first withdrawn during the first fifty years of the second century and then restored," based on the complete absence of any specific evidence; and (2) that later patristic claims of miracles differ from those of the NT, both as to their nature and the mode of their working. Later claims of miraculous activity do not yield to clear eye-witness certainty or empirical demonstration as do the NT miracles. All these conclusions point to the fact that the revelation (the purpose of the miracles) was completed with the writing of the 27 books of the NT.

The Lord's church is committed to the final authority of the written word itself. This is public truth and is definite and clear. Regardless of what any person may claim about working any miracle today or receiving any communication, revelation, signal or message today, we have to reject this as clearly contrary to the teaching of the NT, which is our certain authoritative revelation. Any man who claims new present-day revelation necessarily repudiates the NT as his authority in religion when he does so. He also repudiates the facts of history.

It should be emphasized that the claims of miracle-working among Pentecostal groups in recent years are not found in the major streams of "Christianity" back over the past two thousand years. These people should explain why this gap, if this power was supposed to have been in the church throughout its history.

2 Tim. 3:16, 17 says the scripture is "inspired" and "profitable" for certain helps, "that the man of God may be adequate" ("complete, furnished completely" ARV) "unto every good work."

2 Pet. 1:3—"seeing that His divine power has granted to us everything pertaining to life and godliness . . ."

Jude 3—"contend earnestly for the faith which was once for all delivered to the saints."

Rev. 22:18, 19 say that we must neither "add to" nor "take from the words of the book of this prophecy."

The above passages would be difficult to explain on the thesis that revelation still occurs. There is an all-sufficiency about the NT that defies any man to attempt to write *new scripture* after the inspiration and canonization process was providentially completed.

The New Testament is conscious of itself as a new book of scripture in that 1 Timothy 5:18 quotes Matt. 10:10 and Luke 10:7 as "scripture," and which quotations are not found in the OT. 2 Pet. 3:16 classifies Paul's writings with the "other scriptures," and in 2 Cor. 3:6, 14 Paul recognizes a "New Testament" or covenant as something that can be read.

By using the completed written word we "walk by faith and not by sight" (2 Cor. 5:7). If we today could get new revelation or certain communications from above, we could *know* that it was God's will and would not need to have "faith" in it. Faith has its rightful place in the Christian system—to appropriate the revealed message and to put it to practice in our lives. If in our day we received new and certain revelation from God, the Bible could be ignored.

The doctrine of new revelation, after the cessation of miracles and inspiration (about 100 A.D.), must be classified with the traditions of Catholicism, the *Book of Mormon, Science and Health with Key to the Scriptures* and other similar claims as non-valid. The New Testament is the complete, and only authoritative revelation during the Christian dispensation after the cessation of miracles. According to its teaching no other valid message comes from God to man.

Review   Questions

Chapter   9

1. Prove from the New Testament the purpose for which miraculous gifts were given.

2. When did miracles cease? What New Testament passages show this?

3. Interpret "the perfect" in 1 Cor. 13:10. Comment on the time of "partial knowledge" and then of "complete knowledge" in the early church.

4. Identify: "Infancy;" "childhood;" "maturity;" "full-grownness." Are all these to deal with the earth-life of the church, or are the latter two to be fulfilled in heaven? Why?

5. Give four or five major conclusions from Warfield's book.

6. Are present day claims for supernatural pwoers based on subjective or objective evidence? What support does this give to validity?

7. Give the New Testament evidence indicating that revelation has been final since the first century.

Chapter 10

THE CHARISMATIC MOVEMENT — NEO-PENTECOSTALISM

As the last chapter indicated, the charismatic gifts (miracles, etc.) ceased at the close of the apostolic age and this comports not only with NT teaching but also with the evidence of history. After a time when there was neither evidence nor claims for miracles, they began to be claimed again, but, as Warfield observed, they were not obvious, specific or definite nor were they verifiable publicly like the miracles of the NT record. The question concerning these later claims is, were they a bonafide continuation of the NT charismata, or were they purely psychological phenomena?

The group known as Montanists (about the middle of the second century, A.D.) were among the earliest non-canonical claimants to the power of miraculous gifts, including tongue-speaking. Montanus was also probably the world's most radical premillennialist of all time and was considered as so unorthodox that his whole movement was considered heretical within the second century. Irenaeus, late in the second century, mentions gifts, and even the gift of speaking in "all kinds of languages," though not of "speaking in tongues." Warfield and some others feel that likely Irenaeus was really discussing what went on in NT days rather than in his own day, and there is also some possibility that he referred to Montanist claims. Tertullian speaks favorably of gifts, but he had himself joined the Montanists. Both Chrysostom and Augustine observe that there were no *glossolalia* (tongue speakings) in their day. Authors covering the middle ages indicate a relative absence of claims of glossolalia for this entire period. There are some references to it in more recent times among the Mormons, among some of the converts of Whitefield and Wesley and among certain other groups, but it is notably infrequent and where claimed it was among the minority groups rather than in the major segments of "Christendom."

For those who claim that tongue-speaking was divinely intended to be a normal part of continuing Christianity throughout the ages there is an obligation for them to show why it appeared so spasmodically and so seldom. The voice of history seems to deny their claim, even if they could show that what is claimed is the real thing.

The original Pentecostal movements had their beginning about 1900 and their distinctive teachings emphasized the use of glossolalia, as well as the baptism of the Holy Spirit, entire sanctification as "a second work of grace," and certain other definite views.

Neo-Pentecostalism is a designation which has been applied to the recent spread of the use of glossolalia among the larger and more dignified, "established" churches. This aspect began with an Episcopal minister in California, and now affects Presbyterians, Reformed Church of America, some Lutherans, Methodists, Baptists, and Catholics, and it has been taken up among certain youth groups of interdenominational character. It has affected some in the church of Christ. It warrants full investigation.

Among the Pentecostals the "gift of tongues" is normally considered as evidence that one has received the baptism, though not always. The gift serves two purposes—for private devotions ("self-edification"), and congregational use, where "interpretation" may be expected. Pentecostals are fairly well agreed that the tongues of Acts 2 are actual foreign languages, but they differ as to the nature of those of 1 Cor. 14, possibly the majority holding that they are rather the speaking of an "heavenly language," unknown to man; while others accept these as also actual human languages, though perhaps not even comprehended by the speaker. Present-day glossolalia are also identified as both of these types, with some Pentecostals acknowledging that some of the efforts are fraudulent.

Since there is no standard of authority for the various Neo-Pentecostal expressions it is difficult to assess them with a firm interpretation, though it should be observed that they are an out-growth of the original Pentecostalism itself and ultimately must be interpreted in this light. The Neo-Pentecostals argue as to whether tongues are an indispensable evidence of the baptism of the Spirit, though probably most of them accept this as true. Generally Neo-Pentecostals are less emotional than Pentecostals, and do not encourage the practice at the more dignified of their public services.

The cause of the recent expansion and flurry in the use of glossolalia has been attributed to a reaction against the lack of spirituality in some churches in favor of logic and ritualistic ceremony. This may be partially justifiable. Of course no amount of failure on one person's part is justification for someone else to adopt any unscriptural teaching, but certainly the people of God should be strongly God-conscious and should be very spiritually minded. We should be strong believers in prayer and should be praying people, fully aware that God hears and answers. We should be fervent in worship and should, indeed, be filled with the Spirit (Eph. 5:18).

A Biblical Evaluation

The following categories have been offered as classifications of tongue-speaking phenomena: (1) Actual foreign languages, unknown to the speaker but knowable by an interpreter or known by at least some of his hearers. This usage served for preaching the gospel by inspiration without having first to learn the language, as present-day missionaries are required to do. The tongues of Acts 2 are accepted even by Pentecostals as illustrating this category. It is this writer's feeling that this is the only type of tongue-speaking described anywhere in the NT.

(2) Some hold that the glossolalia of 1 Cor. 14 were actual languages, but for a different purpose from that of Acts 2—namely, self-edification. They also see a difference in that the Acts incident seems to be a once-for-all event while the Corinthian manifestation was a repeatable one. Again, they say in 1 Cor. 14 an interpreter was required, and, only a few had this gift, whereas in Acts 2 all in the group seemed to be able to use the gift. It is the insistence of this author that all of these "differences" are invalid. They were actual human languages, which sometimes needed an interpreter (apparently some speakers could speak in specific languages but not in others—1 Cor. 13:27,28). They served for self-edification only if the speaker could interpret in his own language. It was the *baptism* that was once-for-all in Acts, not the speaking in tongues. The latter were repeatable in Acts as well as in Corinthians. In any worship service (other than the apostles and at Cornelius' household) only certain ones could use the gifts. The term "foreign language" or "unknown actual human language" can be used in every instance in 1 Cor. 14 as a substitute for the word *tongues*, and it will make perfect sense in every case.

(3) A third category for the term glossolalia is what seems to be an "ecstatic jabber"—no actual human language, but if a language at all it would be a "heavenly" one—of which we have no verification whatever. The person uttering this ecstatic jargon might

be only under an intense psychological pressure and really be saying nothing at all. He has no way of being sure.

We insist that Category No. 1 above is the true explanation of "tongues" in the NT, and that they, like all miracles, served only the purpose of getting the true gospel preached and taught to the people. Tongues (foreign languages) were not to be used in public services unless there was an interpreter present— confusion was condemned (1 Cor. 14:28; 33; 40). Modern "tongue-speaking" public services violate this principle of "confusion" completely and would not be approved of God—even if they were the real thing! There is not only no NT authority for tongue-speaking today, but it would be contradictory to God's will (as 1 Cor. 14 teaches) as it is now practiced in public services of both the Pentecostals and the Neo-Pentecostals.

Psychology

Dr. Stuart Bergsma's little booklet *(Baker's, Grand Rapids, Mich.,) reflects an interesting study concerning the physiology and psychology of this phenomenon. Bergsma is a practicing psychiatrist who has strong theological interests and who has studied this problem in great detail. His analysis and conclusions about modern glossolalia as a purely psychological phenomenon (his field of competence) are rather clear and precise.

Bergsma first points out that physiologically, the human brain is somewhat similar to a computer, though more intricate. If a computer is overloaded, however, it will become erratic and will demonstrate "neurotic" symptoms, acting like it is "possessed of demons," and thus "may spew out nonsense if pushed beyond its limits" (p. 13). By the same token, the human brain has limits—

*Quotations by permission.

and under high emotional strain may "rattle off nonsense syllables, broken phrases, pseudo language" (p. 13).

Bergsma notes that "almost without exception authors writing on modern glossolalia and psychologists studying glossolalists, regard the phenomenon as a neurotic manifestation" (p. 15). We quote him further:

> Cutten (4) mentions the hysteria; the ecstasy of emotion based on the lack of normal self-control; the personality disintegration, which is temporary (during speech); the take-over of the speech or word center with the subject under the control, not of his rational higher cortical centers but in the control of and obedient to subconscious function; the automatic behavior, the approach of all these resulting phenomena to actual psychosis with visual and auditory hallucinations; the tremendous power which suggestion by leaders has, and the power the expectation of the audience has, on the glossolalist; the progression from inarticulate sounds and grunts to articulate sounds which simulate words; then, as practice grows, to fabrication of words and coined words and articulate speech using formed words, and disconnected foreign words of which the speaker himself is not even conscious that he has a memory of the words; all resulting in a production that is unintelligible to both speaker and audience. In fact the incomprehensibility is an asset, it is maintained; it proves the genuineness, for nothing else would prove that this is really the Holy Spirit who speaks and not a man! (p. 15).
>
> Drummond . . . stresses the facilitation by practice; believes it a hypnotic passive state, with controls inhibited; that loosening of controls of the speech center, or damage of it, can result in increased speech, uncontrolled. A subconscious which is soaked in religion will relate the confused speech to religion, and that person will feel he is motivated to speak because the Holy Spirit is laboring to get free and communicate through him to others . . . It "feels so good" to be speaking thus. The speaker takes the shortcut of a reflex action, bringing a dissociation upon himself, by which the words do not go before the rational cerebral cortex for inspection, reflection and judgment as to whether they make sense, but are sent out directly by the efferent nerves as speech (p. 16).
>
> Bess . . . states the drawing power of the glossolalia movement among the present day intellectual types is the unconscious need all people have to solve their personality

conflicts, to shed their feelings of inadequacy and guilt. Glossolalia gives such folk "instant coffee" (p. 16).

Geddes . . . makes an interesting comparison of the "symptoms" of glossolalia with those induced by "LSD" . . . LSD, the drug lysergic acid, when administered to human experimental subjects, temporarily induces syndromes similar to schizophrenia. So does glossolalia, he maintains, as both cause a deep, profound, soul-shaking experience. Glossolalists have told him it is like getting spiritual maturity for nothing . . . Both of them have the same look in their eyes, their primitive self or id has been released and he considers this can be dangerous (p. 17).

From the above it is easy to realize that the "symptoms" of glossolalia can be produced by something other than an actual gift of the Holy Spirit. There are natural explanations!

As to motivations, Bergsma says:

Many religious minds yearn for a closer contact with God, for a more intimate contact with the Holy Spirit . . . Identification with leaders in a group is psychologically very compelling. Religion with action, be it one that promises voices, visions, miracles, or the reward of becoming a person distinguished by almost supernatural powers of special access to the Holy Spirit by conversation in ecstasy conferred on only some of the flock, is alluring to many a mind. One is a member of an inner circle. One is looked upon with awe. Honor and respect become one's portion (p. 17).

Especially to a religious person denied other attainments, low on the totem pole as to education or scholastic attainment, whose opinion is seldom asked in spiritual affairs, it is a distinct triumph for him to learn that he can speak in tongues . . . There is the stimulus of the group, the expectation, the highly pleasurable excitement, the exultation as the urge to speak becomes almost intolerable (p. 18).

The words begin to come. One is at first aware of the sonorous cadence, the almost poetic rush of syllables, the onomatopoeia, the thrill like the first plane ride and we are lifting off the ground, we are up, we have lost contact with earth and reality. the glossolalist is now in a dissociative phase, unless he's an absolute fraud or consciously staging an act. Most glossolalists remember nothing of this phase; it is a pathological condition a neurotic condition in which anxieties are gone, the burdens and cares of this world are banished, one's psyche is like an interested spectator watching a parade going past down

> there, while one ecstatically talks to the Holy Spirit in mysteries one neither comprehends nor understands nor remembers later. If pathology can be such bliss, 'tis folly to be normal, non-glossolalic! (p. 18).

It is not to be denied that those who have come to believe that they are glossolalics could have had a dynamic experience, and one which they could easily feel to be a genuine gift of the Spirit. What can be denied, however, is that such is in harmony with NT teaching on the subject. Undoubtedly they may have had a psychological or emotional lift, but this fact is no proof that their basic claim is true. They could well be deluded.

Our Attitude

What should the attitude of the rest of us be toward these, of our number or from outside the church? Obviously it should be one of loving, patient teaching.

Review   Questions

Chapter   10

1. What was the general picture and attitude concerning miraculous gifts in the second century A.D.?

2. How is the term "tongues" variously defined?

3. Why cannot one be sure that glossolalia today are genuine, when one could be sure in New Testament times?

4. Since the New Testament gifts were "to confirm the word," what is the most likely New Testament meaning of "tongues?"

5. Comment on Dr. Bergsma's assessment that "tongues" today are *naturally* induced rather than supernaturally.

6. Do Bergsma's "motivations" seem adequate?

Chapter 11

SUMMARY AND OBSERVATIONS

By way of summary, we note that there are several different expressions or ways through which the Holy Spirit influenced people in early Christian times, some of which are still valid and operative today—the inspired word, by the personal indwelling, and providence. These might all be in use at the same time with respect to a given individual. There is no New Testament evidence favoring today's peculiar doctrines about the Spirit such as the baptism, direct operation in conversion, or miracles, including tongue speaking. The New Testament does not teach continuing revelation, but both it and the facts of history indicate that revelation has long since ceased. We conclude, therefore, that *there is no new revelation today*, no new knowledge, facts, information, signals or communication from God's mind to human minds. His revelation for us today is completely contained in the Bible. There is, however, abundant providential activity going on, applicable even to special individuals and groups, whereas revelation is available to all equally. Providence, however, is not open or evident. No man *knows* whether God helps him providentially or answers his prayer. He may well *believe* that a given event was such an action, though he cannot absolutely confirm it.

The word and the personal Spirit act conjointly in many matters. The Spirit is due credit for all of the word's influence, since it is His "sword." However, the

73

Spirit can act and can influence people in other ways than through the word. The Spirit gives *revelation* to alien sinners only through the word, though He may act providentially with respect to them such as arranging for a meeting with a preacher (as in the cases of the eunuch and Cornelius). Never does the Spirit force a decision or overrule a person's own choice, however. Any man who chooses for Christ or makes a moral decision does so as a free agent. There is no depravity to be removed and the word itself has inherent spiritual power to produce a free, rational and deliberate choice of believing on Christ.

Providence is abundant. God cares for us individually and guarantees to see the faithful through to success and victory (Romans 8:26-39). The Spirit is active in providence though we have no revelation as to how providence specifically works.

The *how* of the Spirit's indwelling is both *personal* and *through the word*. He is personally given as a gift to the Christian at baptism, to serve as a seal of identification and as a *pledge* of future inheritance. The Spirit bears witness with our spirits that we are children of God. From within our hearts (because we are sons), the personal Spirit cries, "Abba! Father!" (Gal. 4:6). The Spirit "was not yet given" before Jesus' glorification (John 7:38, 39), but He is today promised to every penitent baptized believer (Acts 2:38). Our bodies become the temples in which He dwells. He is given only to those who obey (Acts 5:32), but is not given to cause people to obey! We know of His presence in us only through faith in the teachings of the word.

The Spirit leads Christians through the teaching of the word, but also providentially. The latter is a non-revelatory, "behind the scenes" action and is never obvious nor certain. He helps us to "put to death the deeds of the body," "pours out the love of God in our hearts," and "helps our infirmities."

There is ample evidence from the New Testament and from history that revelation ceased about the time of the writing of the New Testament. Those who claim later revelations have the burden of proof and they have no evidence to support their claims; whereas, the New Testament *Charismata* were open and evident miracles— "public truth." Today's claims are only subjective and private and are non-convincing. This is true of today's "tongue speaking" claims. The observable phenomena can be explained as naturalistic in origin. The tongue-talker has no way of even being sure himself that he is having a supernatural experience. In New Testament days, however, even the skeptics had to admit that the miracles were genuine. Back then, nobody doubted the reality of the miracle. In fact, this was the purpose of the miracle—to remove doubt. It really couldn't be a miracle if it were not clearly evident to all that the supernatural was present. It would appear that the Pentecostals and Neo-Pentecostals thus are self-deluded.

Observations

There is no reason to believe that non-Christians have the promise of the Spirit, nor can they claim His providential aid. Successes of false religious teachers can be credited only to applied psychology—not to the idea of "God working with them," or "the leading of the Spirit."

For Christians, however, there is much aid promised. Our relation to the Spirit is close. We have "fellowship" (*koinonia*) with the Holy Spirit (2 Cor. 13:14); we can be "filled with the Holy Spirit" (Acts 13:52; Eph. 5:18); we can "abound in hope through the power of the Holy Spirit" (Rom. 15:13); and our inner man can be "strengthened with power through His Spirit" (Eph. 3:16). When we become Christians, we are "joined to the Lord" (1 Cor. 6:16, 17), and our spirits become "one Spirit" with Him in a spiritual union or marriage. God "is near to each one of us" (Acts 17:27), and "causes all things to work together for good" for us (Rom. 8:28). He "is at work in *us* (you), both to will and to work for His good pleasure" (Phil. 2:13), and He providentially "opens doors" for the word to His preachers (Col. 4:3; Acts 14:27; 1 Cor. 16:9). Paul said, "I can do all things through Him who strengthens me" (Phil. 4:13), and the context indicates that this is true for all Christians, not just apostles or for the age of miracles. We need to realize fully that people are primarily spirit beings, with spiritual opportunities, obligations, and blessings. God guarantees victory to the man of faith, and furnishes adequate strength for the purpose as long as he continues strong in faith.

When church problems arise, some members tend to get caught up in emotional aspects based on friendships, reputations, or reasons other than logic and rational study of the cold, straight teachings. Often times, we do not have access to all the facts, but we go ahead and reach conclusions anyway. We are prone to climb up on somebody's "band-wagon" without knowing all the reasons or implications involved. In short, we form factions, with party spirit and party attitudes, and thus become guilty of being schismatic to some degree or other. We ought to be careful about doing or saying anything that might contribute to a cleavage between brethren. "Let not many *of you* become teachers, my brethren, knowing that as such we shall incur a stricter judgment" (James 3:1).

We still feel that the differences between Christians today over the doctrine of the Holy Spirit are not as much as some seem to think. Seemingly, one "cluster of opinion," the "word only" group, believes that those arguing for personal indwelling would "throw the gate open" to present day revelation, Holy Spirit baptism, miracles, tongue-speaking, etc., when in reality they would accept none of these things. The current tongue speaking phenomenon did not start with a strong

76

impetus and only a comparative few are caught up in it. Likely, these have accepted a strong psychological impact for the "supernatural" as they sought aid for personal problems. On the other hand, some of those who accept the personal indwelling and a strong providence seem to feel that the "word only" brethren are so mechanical in outlook that they deny answer to prayer, providence, deep spirituality, etc., when in reality they also accept all of these things. Both groups seem to be scared of each other's views, and have not been giving full credit for views actually held. Though there are some real differences, we all can "be brethren" in the fullest sense. With patience, study and brotherly love, we can work out any of these problems.

Review   Questions

Chapter   11

1. Name the special influences of the Holy Spirit in the early days of Christianity that are no longer with us. Name some that are.

2. Indicate ways that the Spirit and the word work conjointly.

3. Can providence work through the word?

4. Does the Spirit ever act irresistibly, or is man always free to choose and thus be responsible for his choices?

5. What is a prime difference between the New Testament charismatic gifts and those claimed for today?

6. What assurance can a tongue-talker today have that his actions are supernatural in origin and not just natural?

7. Mention some things from the New Testament that indicate that we can have a closeness with God and that He works in us.

Chapter 12

SPIRITUALITY

Spirituality is a requisite of true New Testament Christianity (Gal. 6:1; Col. 1:9). It is our obligation as teachers of the word to carry on a continuing, total "war against *spiritual* poverty. It is not enough that we should "make disciples of all nations," but we are also commanded to teach "them to observe all that I commanded you" (Matt. 28:19, 20). There are *second principles* to Christianity as well as first principles (see Heb. 6:1). We must "grow in grace and knowledge" and become "spiritually minded" in order to be fully pleasing to God.

Spirituality involves depth understanding of God's revelation and full appreciation of its teaching and of spiritual values and relationships. It includes a knowledge of God and His ways, a personal acquaintance with Christ, and an understanding and full appreciation of the person of the Holy Spirit and His activities. It is not possible to achieve the highest in spirituality with false doctrines about any of these. Truth is paramount, and nobody's tradition can replace the New Testament word. "To the books and to the testimony" must ever be our determination as truth-seekers!

The doctrines of the personal indwelling of the Spirit and a strong providential activity aid our own spiritual development toward its highest potential. Though the age of miracles is over, spiritual relationships and spiritual activities are not over! The awareness that the third member of the Godhead personally and actually dwells within us is a tremendous incentive to holiness. A deep faith in God's frequent and continuing providential care makes us stronger in faith and gives us a greater appreciation for our relation to Him, and for other spiritual values also.

I once knew a man who could argue scripture well but who, in a Sunday-school class discussion, stated that he did not believe that God would actually hear and answer prayer. We were astounded at such an admission because he prayed long and loudly in the worship services. I asked him that if he did not believe that prayers received God's attention and produced action on His part, why did he ever pray in the first place? His answer was another shocker. "Because I'm commanded to," he replied. This is the most radical case of legalism that I have personally encountered, before or since. For him Christianity was only "rule-keeping," and was completely devoid of spirituality, spiritual growth, spiritual relationships and spiritual values. "Law and obedience" (or clock-punching) was for him all there is to it. He had no sensitivity for person to person communion or fellowship of the Christian with the Godhead—religion being purely the mechanical business of keeping God appeased. There was for him no "love which casts out fear," only the fear!

Only by realizing that there are in Christianity such concerns as love, person to person spiritual relationships, a closeness to God in our daily walk, and the availability of abundant individual and personal help can we get the most out of Christianity. And if we do not reflect an awareness of these the effectiveness of our preaching to others will be curtailed.

Most all congregations of the Lord's church have many members who do not attend Bible study, Sunday night service or midweek prayer meeting. Rare is the congregation that has as many at Sunday evening services as at the Sunday morning service. We've even recently heard of arguments about "essential services" versus "non-essential services." We should face it—all this indicates that many of our people are only "clock-punchers," legalists, who have little love and little spirituality yet who are strong on "obedience" to a minimum of commands. Their understanding of the Christian system is more mechanical than truly spiritual. We can never take the world for Christ until we ourselves become more spiritually minded. We need a full grasp of being "saved by grace through faith" (Eph. 2:8) and of what it means "to be crucified with Christ"; and, "it is no longer I that live, but Christ lives in me" (Gal. 2:20).

Needed Emphases

An important source of spirituality is the word. It edifies us and builds us up in the holy faith. It furnishes information that enables us to grow in needed spiritual knowledge. It makes us conscious of the opportunity for personal fellowship and communion with the Godhead. Spiritually minded persons can be strongly God-conscious—of His nearness to us and of His personal interest in us. They can be aware of being sealed with the Spirit, of being given Him as a pledge or down payment of future salvation and of His personal presence as a guest in their bodies. They can learn that "because we are sons" the Spirit in our hearts cries, "Abba! Father!"—that we have received "a spirit of adoption as sons by which we also can cry out, "Abba! Father!"—and that "the Spirit Himself bears witness with our spirit that we are children of God." All such awareness aids the development of our individual spirituality.

The Spirit helps our weaknesses and prays or intercedes for us in ways that are beyond our understanding (Rom. 8:26). To recognize and believe that this is a constant and continuing actuality is not to have the "mind of the flesh," but the "mind of the spirit" which leads to "life and peace" and to "joy unspeakable and full of glory."

The "person to person" communion that Christians have in worship furnishes spiritual strength and develops our spirituality. The consciousness that Christ is actually present and participates with us in the communion cannot but build us spiritually. To "pray at all times in the Spirit" (Eph. 6:18) for "boldness" (v. 19), for "wisdom" (James 1:5), or for anything else means that we have more in Christianity than mere "mechanics."

We are saved by grace, but it is not a cheap grace (costing us nothing). It is rather an expensive grace, costing us our total selves. This is a paradox but both aspects are true. Salvation is free but yet costs us everything. We are saved by atonement, not attainment—yet our faith must be a working faith. We believe rather than achieve, as the ground of salvation, yet obedience is a necessary ingredient of saving faith.

May we more and more come to appreciate Paul's prayer for us—that we may "be strengthened with power through His Spirit in the inner man" . . . and "know the love of Christ which surpasses knowledge," and "be filled up to all the fulness of God" (Eph. 3:16, 19).

Review   Questions

Chapter   12

1. Define "spirituality." Describe it at its highest.

2. Do understandings of correct doctrines influence our spirituality?

3. What does a legalistic, mechanical attitude do to deep spirituality?

4. On the other side of the coin—what does an emotional, non-Biblical attitude that relies on feelings do to a real spirituality?

5. Why must the word and its teachings be our final control?

6. Can one have happiness if he is deeply spiritual while being governed by the word?